WRITE IT ALL OUT. EVERYTHING.

ALL YOUR THOUGHTS, FEARS, WINS.

**This Journal Belongs to:**

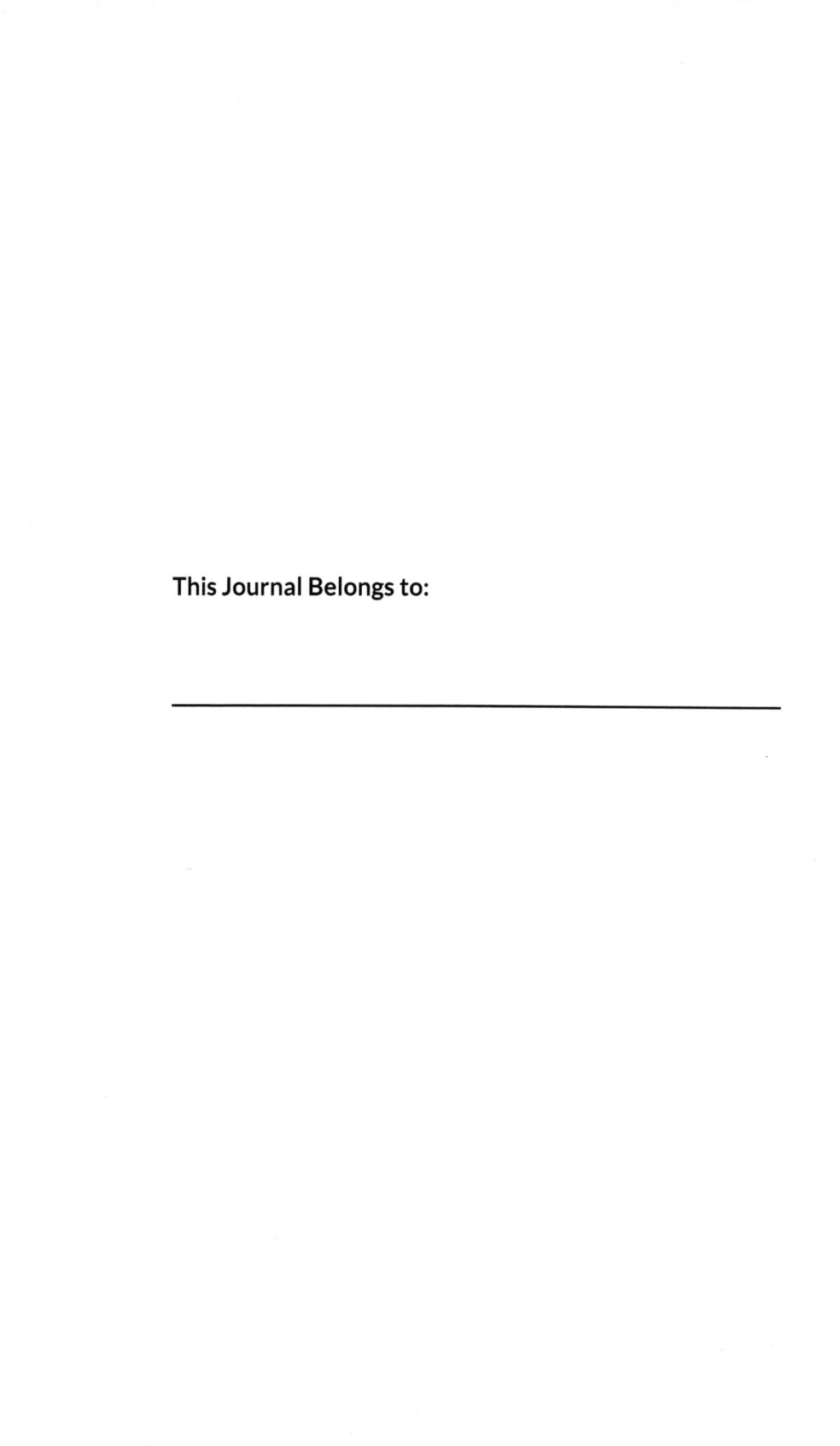

_____

**She Believed She Could & Sooo She Did,** charges you to write out your wins. Release your thoughts onto the blank, ruled pages and let go of their hold over you. Write down all of the reasons that woke you up and helped you make it through the day.

> IF YOU LOVE THE USE OF THIS JOURNAL AS MUCH AS I KNOW YOU WILL, PLEASE LEAVE AN AMAZON REVIEW SO OTHERS CAN LOVE IT, TOO! THANK YOU FOR YOUR CONTINUED SUPPORT.
>
> — E Michelle

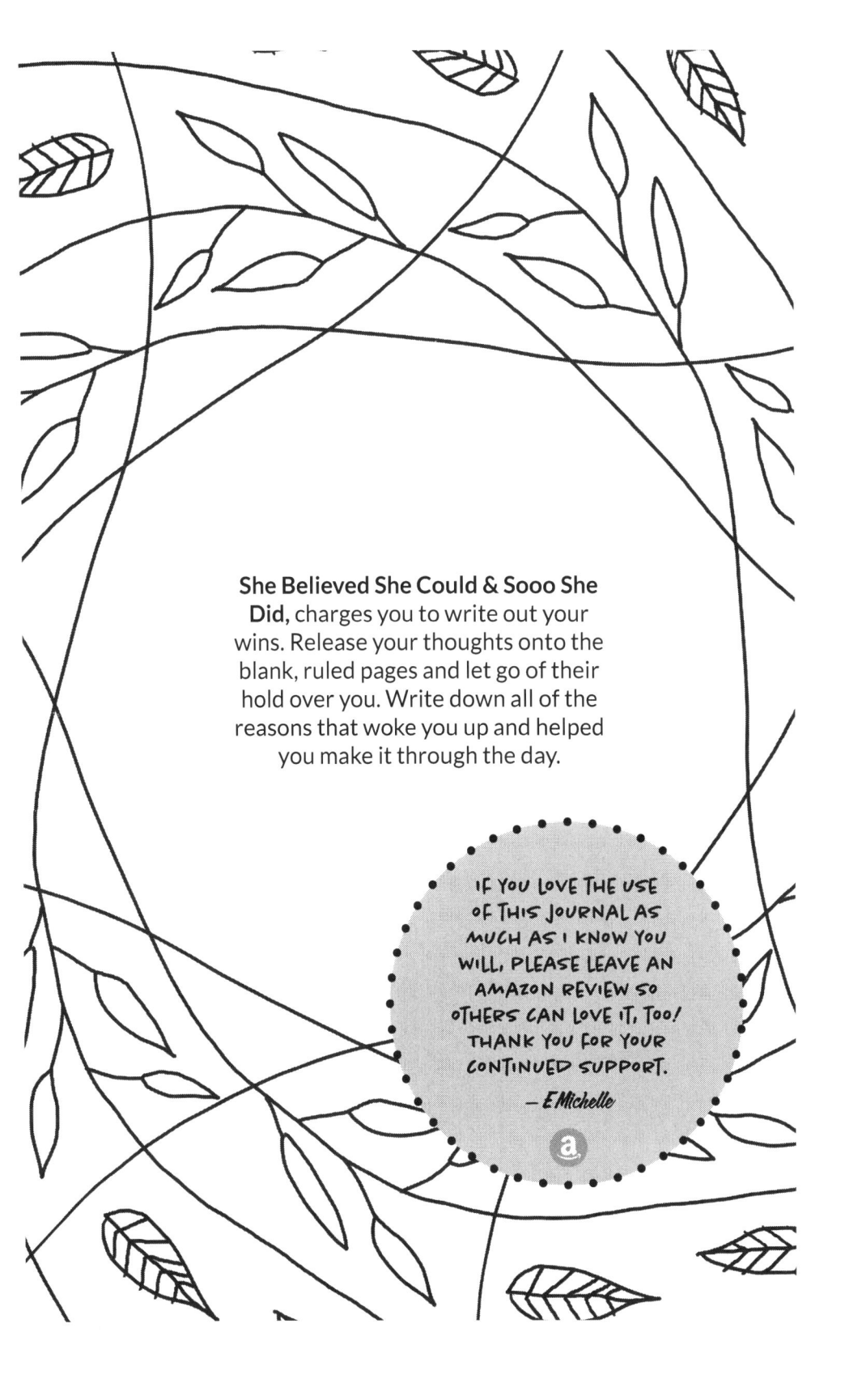

SHE BELIEVED SHE COULD

AND SOOO SHE DID

SHE BELIEVED SHE COULD

AND SOOO SHE DID

SHE BELIEVED SHE COULD

AND SOOO SHE DID

SHE BELIEVED SHE COULD

AND SOOO SHE DID

SHE BELIEVED SHE COULD

AND SOOO SHE DID

SHE BELIEVED SHE COULD

AND SOOO SHE DID

SHE BELIEVED SHE COULD

AND SOOO SHE DID

SHE BELIEVED SHE COULD

AND SOOO SHE DID

SHE BELIEVED SHE COULD

AND SOOO SHE DID

SHE BELIEVED SHE COULD

AND SOOO SHE DID

SHE BELIEVED SHE COULD

AND SOOO SHE DID

SHE BELIEVED SHE COULD

AND SOOO SHE DID

SHE BELIEVED SHE COULD

AND SOOO SHE DID

SHE BELIEVED SHE COULD

AND SOOO SHE DID

SHE BELIEVED SHE COULD

AND SOOO SHE DID

SHE BELIEVED SHE COULD

AND SOOO SHE DID

SHE BELIEVED SHE COULD

AND SOOO SHE DID

SHE BELIEVED SHE COULD

AND SOOO SHE DID

SHE BELIEVED SHE COULD

AND SOOO SHE DID

SHE BELIEVED SHE COULD

AND SOOO SHE DID

SHE BELIEVED SHE COULD

AND SOOO SHE DID

SHE BELIEVED SHE COULD

AND SOOO SHE DID

SHE BELIEVED SHE COULD

AND SOOO SHE DID

SHE BELIEVED SHE COULD

AND SOOO SHE DID

SHE BELIEVED SHE COULD

AND SOOO SHE DID

SHE BELIEVED SHE COULD

AND SOOO SHE DID

SHE BELIEVED SHE COULD

AND SOOO SHE DID

SHE BELIEVED SHE COULD

AND SOOO SHE DID

SHE BELIEVED SHE COULD

AND SOOO SHE DID

SHE BELIEVED SHE COULD

AND SOOO SHE DID

SHE BELIEVED SHE COULD

AND SOOO SHE DID

SHE BELIEVED SHE COULD

AND SOOO SHE DID

SHE BELIEVED SHE COULD

AND SOOO SHE DID

SHE BELIEVED SHE COULD

AND SOOO SHE DID

SHE BELIEVED SHE COULD

AND SOOO SHE DID

SHE BELIEVED SHE COULD

AND SOOO SHE DID

SHE BELIEVED SHE COULD

AND SOOO SHE DID

SHE BELIEVED SHE COULD

AND SOOO SHE DID

SHE BELIEVED SHE COULD

AND SOOO SHE DID

SHE BELIEVED SHE COULD

AND SOOO SHE DID

SHE BELIEVED SHE COULD

AND SOOO SHE DID

SHE BELIEVED SHE COULD

AND SOOO SHE DID

SHE BELIEVED SHE COULD

AND SOOO SHE DID

SHE BELIEVED SHE COULD

AND SOOO SHE DID

SHE BELIEVED SHE COULD

AND SOOO SHE DID

SHE BELIEVED SHE COULD

AND SOOO SHE DID

SHE BELIEVED SHE COULD

AND SOOO SHE DID

SHE BELIEVED SHE COULD

AND SOOO SHE DID

SHE BELIEVED SHE COULD

AND SOOO SHE DID

SHE BELIEVED SHE COULD

AND SOOO SHE DID

SHE BELIEVED SHE COULD

AND SOOO SHE DID

SHE BELIEVED SHE COULD

AND SOOO SHE DID

SHE BELIEVED SHE COULD

AND SOOO SHE DID

SHE BELIEVED SHE COULD

AND SOOO SHE DID

SHE BELIEVED SHE COULD

AND SOOO SHE DID

SHE BELIEVED SHE COULD

AND SOOO SHE DID

SHE BELIEVED SHE COULD

AND SOOO SHE DID

SHE BELIEVED SHE COULD

AND SOOO SHE DID

SHE BELIEVED SHE COULD

AND SOOO SHE DID

SHE BELIEVED SHE COULD

AND SOOO SHE DID

SHE BELIEVED SHE COULD

AND SOOO SHE DID

SHE BELIEVED SHE COULD

AND SOOO SHE DID

SHE BELIEVED SHE COULD

AND SOOO SHE DID

SHE BELIEVED SHE COULD

AND SOOO SHE DID

SHE BELIEVED SHE COULD

AND SOOO SHE DID

SHE BELIEVED SHE COULD

AND SOOO SHE DID

SHE BELIEVED SHE COULD

AND SOOO SHE DID

SHE BELIEVED SHE COULD

AND SOOO SHE DID

SHE BELIEVED SHE COULD

AND SOOO SHE DID

SHE BELIEVED SHE COULD

AND SOOO SHE DID

SHE BELIEVED SHE COULD

AND SOOO SHE DID

SHE BELIEVED SHE COULD

AND SOOO SHE DID

SHE BELIEVED SHE COULD

AND SOOO SHE DID

SHE BELIEVED SHE COULD

AND SOOO SHE DID

SHE BELIEVED SHE COULD

AND SOOO SHE DID

SHE BELIEVED SHE COULD

AND SOOO SHE DID

SHE BELIEVED SHE COULD

AND SOOO SHE DID

SHE BELIEVED SHE COULD

AND SOOO SHE DID

SHE BELIEVED SHE COULD

AND SOOO SHE DID

SHE BELIEVED SHE COULD

AND SOOO SHE DID

SHE BELIEVED SHE COULD

AND SOOO SHE DID

SHE BELIEVED SHE COULD

AND SOOO SHE DID

SHE BELIEVED SHE COULD

AND SOOO SHE DID

SHE BELIEVED SHE COULD

AND SOOO SHE DID

SHE BELIEVED SHE COULD

AND SOOO SHE DID

SHE BELIEVED SHE COULD

AND SOOO SHE DID

SHE BELIEVED SHE COULD

AND SOOO SHE DID

SHE BELIEVED SHE COULD

AND SOOO SHE DID

SHE BELIEVED SHE COULD

AND SOOO SHE DID

SHE BELIEVED SHE COULD

AND SOOO SHE DID

SHE BELIEVED SHE COULD

AND SOOO SHE DID

SHE BELIEVED SHE COULD

AND SOOO SHE DID

SHE BELIEVED SHE COULD

AND SOOO SHE DID

SHE BELIEVED SHE COULD

AND SOOO SHE DID

SHE BELIEVED SHE COULD

AND SOOO SHE DID

SHE BELIEVED SHE COULD

AND SOOO SHE DID

SHE BELIEVED SHE COULD

AND SOOO SHE DID

# Thank YOU

Your ongoing support means the the world to me. As we journey through life together, may you find peace and purpose along the way. I hope these journals bring a little piece of joy to your life as you fill the pages with your thoughts & dreams; even your worries and prayers. Make time for yourself today and everyday.

Find journals, prints, & more
available across my online platforms!

*Illustrated Melanin*

Made in the USA
Las Vegas, NV
29 March 2022